Contents

What floats?

Things that **float** stay near the top of the water.

These things float.

Investigations

Floating

Patricia Whitehouse

Raintree

www.raintreepublishers.co.uk
Visit our website to find out more information about **Raintree** books.

To order:
☎ Phone 44 (0) 1865 888112
📠 Send a fax to 44 (0) 1865 314091
💻 Visit the Raintree Bookshop at **www.raintreepublishers.co.uk** to browse our catalogue and order online.

First published in Great Britain by Raintree, Halley Court, Jordan Hill, Oxford OX2 8EJ, part of Harcourt Education.
Raintree is a registered trademark of Harcourt Education Ltd.

Editorial: Nick Hunter and Diyan Leake
Design: Michelle Lisseter
Picture Research: Beth Chisholm
Production: Lorraine Hicks

Originated by Dot Gradations
Printed and bound in China by South China Printing Company

ISBN 1 844 21550 4 (hardback)
07 06 05 04 03
10 9 8 7 6 5 4 3 2 1

ISBN 1 844 21556 3 (paperback)
08 07 06 05 04
10 9 8 7 6 5 4 3 2 1

British Library Cataloguing in Publication Data
Whitehouse, Patricia
Floating
532.2'5
A full catalogue record for this book is available from the British Library.

Acknowledgements
The publishers would like to thank the following for permission to reproduce photographs: Heinemann Library/Que-Net

Cover photograph reproduced with permission of Getty images/Photodisc.

Every effort has been made to contact copyright holders of any material reproduced in this book. Any omissions will be rectified in subsequent printings if notice is given to the publishers.

Some words are shown in bold, **like this**. They are explained in the glossary on page 23.

Some things do not float.

They **sink**.

Does bread float?

Lay a piece of bread on some water.

Does it **float**?

Bread floats when it is **flat**.

Now roll the bread into a ball.

The bread **sinks**.

Changing the shape of the bread changes what happens.

Do rocks float?

Put a big rock in some water.

Does it **float**?

The rock **sinks**.

Big rocks are heavier than water.

Put small rocks in some water.

Do they **float**?

The small rocks **sink**, too.

Even these tiny rocks are heavier than water.

Do jars float?

Put an empty jar with its **lid** on in some water.

Does it **float**?

Air in the jar makes it float.

The lid keeps the air in the jar.

Now take the **lid** off the jar.

Then put the jar in the water.

Water goes into the jar.

Water in the jar makes it **sink**.

Do balls of cotton wool float?

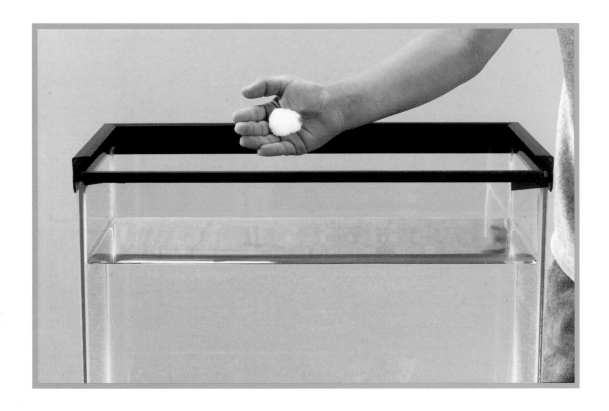

Put a ball of **cotton wool** in some water.

Does it **float?**

There is air inside the cotton wool.

Air makes the ball of cotton
wool float.

Now soak the ball of **cotton wool**.

Put the wet cotton wool in the water.

The cotton wool is now full of water.

Water makes it **sink**.

Quiz

How can you make this bottle **float**?

Look for the answer on page 24.

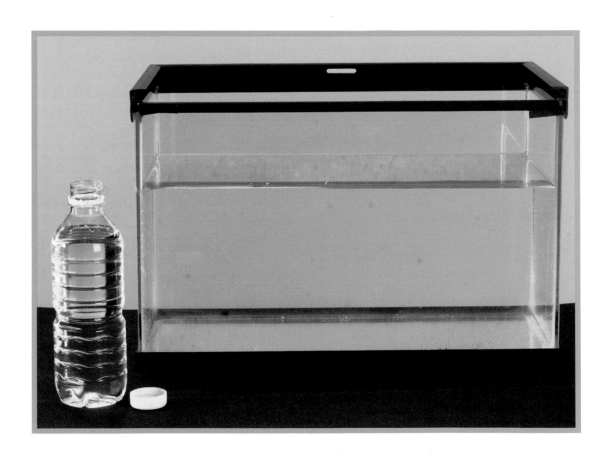

Glossary

cotton wool
soft loose cotton

flat
level and smooth

float
stay on the surface of the water

lid
cover for something, like a jar
or box

sink
go under water and move down
to the bottom

Index

Answer to quiz on page 22

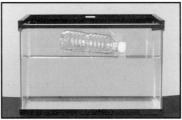

First pour the water out of
the bottle.
Then put the top on.
Air is trapped in the bottle.
Now it will float!

 CAUTION: Children should not attempt any experiment without an adult's
help and permission.